M000086432

Latkes for Sam

by Sarah Hughes
illustrated by Anthony Lewis

CHAPTER 1

All About Latkes

Dad opened the front door. Sam was here for a sleepover!

"Welcome, Sam," said Dad.

"What do you have?" asked Emma.

"It's bread that my mom and I made for breakfast," said Sam. "We can eat it tomorrow morning."

"Great," said Mom. "Thank you!"

"Today we're going to make latkes," said Emma.

"I've never had them before. How do you say it again?" asked Sam.

"We say *lot-kuh,* but some people say *lot-key.* I've heard that both ways are correct," Emma told her.

"There are good things in latkes," said Emma.

"Like what?" asked Sam.

Emma explained, "We use potatoes, onions, oil, eggs, flour, and salt. I eat latkes with applesauce. Mom and Dad like theirs with sour cream. Latkes are so yummy!"

"Mmmm, they do sound yummy," said Sam. "Maybe I'll taste one."

"Good idea," said Mom. She handed Sam an apron.

CHAPTER 2

Making Latkes

"Latkes are our tradition," Dad explained.

"I like to do things the old way," Mom said. "I push the potatoes against the grater, just like your grandma did in Russia, Emma. It's not that difficult."

"First, we shred potatoes, and then we add onions," Dad said.

"Do we mix in the eggs now?" asked Sam.

"Not yet. We have to get all the water out, so we roll the mixture in a towel."

"Everyone has a job," said Emma.

"Yes, nobody is left out," added Sam.

Ben handed Mom a spoon.

"Even Ben!" Mom said, laughing.

8

"I like latkes," said Emma.

"Me too!" said Sam.

"Yum!" said Ben.

CHAPTER 3

Sharing Cultures

The next morning, it was Sam's turn to share food from her culture.

"This is Irish soda bread. They eat it in Ireland. That's where my grandparents were born," said Sam.

"Yum, this is good!" Emma said.

"It's fun to share foods from around the world," Mom said.

"Yum!" said Ben.

"Who wants to split the last piece of bread with me?" asked Dad.

"I do!" Emma and Sam said together.

Respond to Reading

Retell

Use the chart to help you retell *Latkes for Sam.*

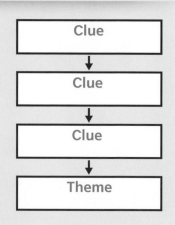

Text Evidence

1. What is the theme of this story?
   Theme

2. How do Sam and Emma feel about the food from each other's culture?
   Theme

3. How do you know that *Latkes for Sam* is realistic fiction? Genre

Compare Texts
Compare how foods are prepared.

WHAT IS A TACO?

A taco is a Mexican meal, but tacos have become very common in the United States. Taco shells can be crunchy or soft. The shell can be filled with meat, cheese, and lots of other foods. Read on to find out how to make a taco!

HOW TO MAKE A TACO

1. Place a taco shell on a plate.

2. Put some meat and beans in the shell.

3. Add cheese.

4. Add some vegetables.

5. Place toppings on the taco. You might like sour cream or sauce.

6. Enjoy!

 Make Connections
What is similar about making tacos and making latkes? Text to Text

15

Focus on Genre

Realistic Fiction Realistic fiction is a story that could be true, but the characters and details are made up.

What to Look for In *Latkes for Sam,* the characters might be like people you know. They make food that your family might make.

Your Turn

Think of a food that is one of your family's traditions. What is in it? When do you eat it? What country is it from? Draw a picture of your family and friends eating the food. Write a few sentences about the food you chose.